Water Bodies

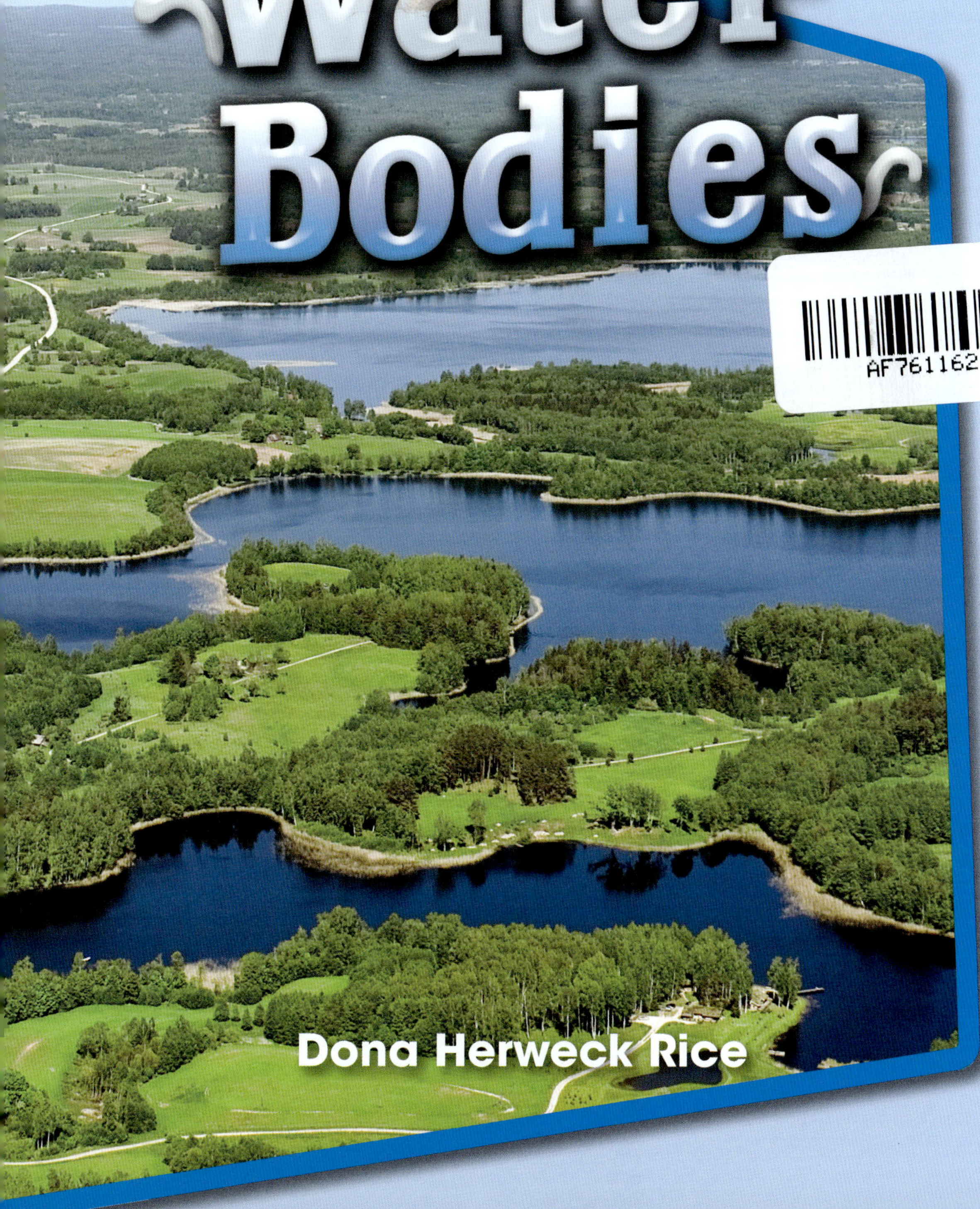

Dona Herweck Rice

Consultants

Sally Creel, Ed.D.
Curriculum Consultant

Leann Iacuone, M.A.T., NBCT, ATC
Riverside Unified School District

Image Credits: p.23 (center) Brian D Cruickshank/ Getty Images; p.6 iStock; pp.10 (top), 11 (top), 19, 23 (bottom) NASA; pp.28–29 (illustrations) Janelle Bell-Martin; all other images from Shutterstock.

Library of Congress Cataloging-in-Publication Data

Rice, Dona, author.
Water bodies / Dona Herweck Rice ; consultants, Sally Creel, Ed.D., curriculum consultant, Leann Iacuone, M.A.T., NBCT, ATC Riverside Unified School District, Jill Tobin, California Teacher of the Year semi-finalist, Burbank Unified School District.
pages cm
Summary: "Did you know that most of Earth is covered with water? Oceans, lakes, and rivers are water bodies on Earth. Lakes and rivers are fresh water. Oceans are saltwater. Living things depend on water for survival." — Provided by publisher.
Audience: K to grade 3.
Includes index.
ISBN 978-1-4807-4609-1 (pbk.)
ISBN 978-1-4807-5076-0 (ebook)
1. Bodies of water—Juvenile literature.
2. Hydrology—Juvenile literature.
3. Water—Juvenile literature. I. Title.
GB662.3.R515 2015
551.4—dc23

Teacher Created Materials
5301 Oceanus Drive
Huntington Beach, CA 92649-1030
http://www.tcmpub.com

ISBN 978-1-4807-4609-1

Table of Contents

A Watery Planet

Splash in it. Wash in it. Swim in it. Drink it. Water is one of the most important things on Earth.

Rainbow trout live in freshwater.

We can't live without it! So, it's a good thing that water is everywhere. Water covers much more than half of Earth. It's even underground.

Look Out Below!

Almost 70% of Earth's freshwater is found in ice caps and glaciers. The other 30% is found underground.

an underground river

What Makes a Water Body?

A water body is any large amount of water. It is mainly on Earth's **surface**. It can be **contained** in one place, like a lake. Or it can move from place to place, like a stream.

You Are Water!

Did you know that water is right where you are right now? It's true! *You* are more than half water. But you are not a water body!

pond
river

Water bodies are formed in **depressed** areas of Earth. Water collects, or pools, there. It may fall as rain. It may fall as snow. It may spring up from below ground.

Water is a liquid. It fills the shape of whatever holds it. It also moves as Earth moves. This can change the shape of a water body.

Drip, Drop, Drip

The amount of water in water bodies is always changing. **Precipitation** (pri-sip-i-TEY-shuhn), such as rain, adds water to them. **Evaporation** decreases the amount of water.

Types of Water Bodies

There are many types of water bodies. Size is one thing that sets them apart. The way water pools or moves also makes them different.

Oceans

Almost all Earth's water is in oceans. These are huge bodies of water. They cover most of Earth. Oceans are made of saltwater. Lots of plants and animals call the ocean home. But people have only seen a small part of the world's oceans.

The Pacific Ocean is the largest ocean in the world.

Mediterranean Sea

Salty Seas

Seas are like oceans. But they are blocked in by land on all or most sides.

Many lionfish call the Pacific Ocean home.

Lakes

A lake is a large body of mainly still water. It is freshwater. That means that it is not salty the way ocean water is. A lake is mainly contained. Rivers and streams flow to or from lakes. They may **feed** the lake. They may empty it.

Lake McDonald has rivers that flow into it and rivers that flow out.

Most lakes are made by nature. Some lakes are made by people. Either way, many people enjoy spending time at lakes.

Big Lake

One-fifth of all freshwater on Earth is in Lake Baikal, one of Earth's largest lakes.

Lake Baikal is in Russia. The lake is 25 million years old!

Ponds

A pond is a small lake. It is made of freshwater. Many plants and animals live there. Frogs and ducks are happy there. It is a common spot for bugs, too.

Wood ducks live in ponds.

More than 1,000 types of animals live in ponds.

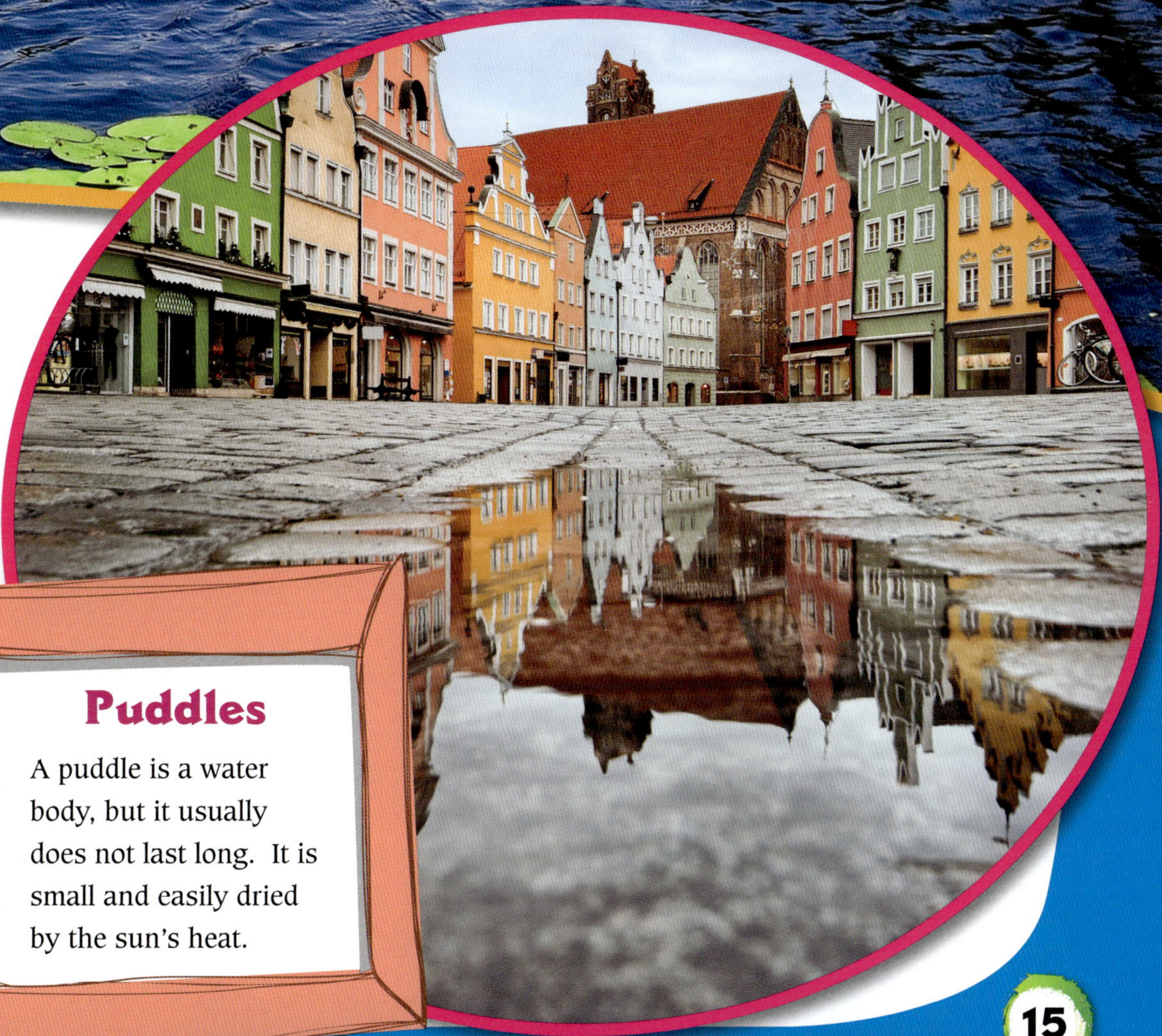

Puddles

A puddle is a water body, but it usually does not last long. It is small and easily dried by the sun's heat.

Wetlands

A wetland is land that is usually soaked with water. The water may not always be there. But it will return. A wetland is filled with plant life. The plants do well in the soggy soil.

Anything Goes!

Water in a wetland can be freshwater or saltwater. Swamps, marshes, and bogs are types of wetlands.

Great willow herbs are flowers that grow in wetlands.

Crawfish are animals that live in swamps.

Rivers

A river is a water body that follows a path. It flows toward a larger body of water. The river may end underground. Or it may dry out. Some rivers are wide. Some are narrow. There are no rules about the size of a river.

Streams

Are streams and rivers different? Not really, although people often think of streams as being smaller than rivers.

River water is usually freshwater.

The Nile River in Egypt is the longest river in the world.

Man-Made

Not every water body is made by nature. People make or reshape some of them.

Waterway

If a body of water is deep enough for a boat to go through, it is called a **waterway**.

canals in Venice, Italy

The Beijing-Hangzhou Grand Canal in China is the longest canal in the world.

Canals

Canals are like rivers. But they are made by people. They can be traveled on in boats. They can also carry water to people. They may be dug where people want a waterway. Or a waterway may be changed to improve it.

A girl carries water on her head after collecting it from Lake Volta.

Reservoirs

Reservoirs (REZ-er-vwahrz) hold and store water. Sometimes, they form in nature. They can be above or below ground. Or people make them. They are mainly behind dams. People do this to control the water. They want to be sure there is water when they need it.

Lake Volta is a reservoir in Ghana. It is the largest reservoir in the world.

Réservoir

The word *reservoir* comes from the French word *réservoir*, which means "storehouse."

The Wonder of Water

Some land features have water. But they are not water bodies. A waterfall is not a water body. It is just a place where water spills. Geysers (GAHY-zerz) are not water bodies. Water just gushes from them.

a waterfall

Old Faithful, in Yellowstone National Park in Wyoming, is one of the most famous geysers in the world.

Old Faithful erupts every 60 to 120 minutes.

No matter what you call water, it is everywhere. Water is important. We need it to live.

Water bodies change all the time. Some may get bigger. Some may evaporate. Who knows? You may be sitting on the home of a great water body yet to come!

These fossilized shells were discovered on land. This means that water used to cover that area.

Let's Do Science!

How do water bodies change? See for yourself!

What to Get

- clay
- sand
- tray
- water

What to Do

1. Fill the tray with clay.

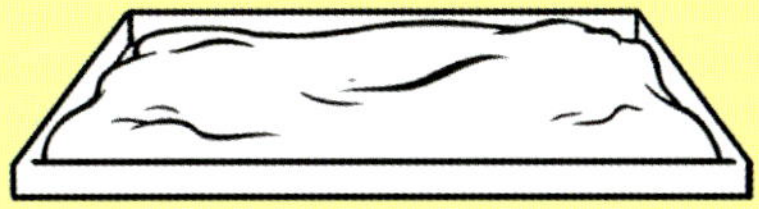

2. Mold the clay to make hills and valleys. Add sand to some areas of the clay.

3. Pour water over some of the clay and sand. Where does the water settle?

4. Gently tip and shake the tray. Add more water. What do you notice when you do these things?

Glossary

contained—held inside

depressed—indented like a hole

evaporation—the process of changing from a liquid to a gas

feed—to give what is needed for continued growth

freshwater—water without salt in it, mainly found in rivers, lakes, and groundwater

precipitation—rain, snow, and other forms of water that fall to Earth

surface—the upper layer of an area of land or water

waterway—a water body deep and wide enough for boats and ships to travel through

Index

Your Turn!

Watching Water

Visit the water body nearest your home. Is it a puddle? A lake? An ocean? What do you see there? What do you hear and smell? Draw a picture of the water body, and write a sentence to describe it.